I0813749

The Essential John Glassco

The Essential John Glassco

selected by Carmine Starnino

The Porcupine's Quill

Library and Archives Canada Cataloguing in Publication

Title: The essential John Glassco / selected by Carmine Starnino.
Other titles: Poems. Selections (Starnino)
Names: Glassco, John, author. | Starnino, Carmine, editor.
Series: Essential poets (Erin, Ont.)
Description: Series statement: Essential poets ; 23 | Poems.
| Includes bibliographical references.
Identifiers: Canadiana (print) 20210328169 | Canadiana (ebook) 20210328193
| ISBN 9780889844421 (softcover) | ISBN 9780889844438 (PDF)
Classification: LCC PS8513.L388 A6 2021 | DDC C811/.54—dc23

1 2 3 • 23 22 21

Published by The Porcupine's Quill, 68 Main Street, PO Box 160,
Erin, Ontario NOB 1T0. http://porcupinesquill.ca

Copyedited by Chandra Wohleber.

Represented in Canada by Canadian Manda.
Trade orders are available from University of Toronto Press.

We acknowledge the support of the Ontario Arts Council and the Canada Council for the Arts for our publishing program. The financial support of the Government of Canada is also gratefully acknowledged.

Table of Contents

Foreword

Unsmiling and seigneurial, John Glassco stares out from the back of his 1971 *Selected Poems*. He is sixty-one. His moustache is trimmed, his ascot crisp; a pampered air attends his expression. 'A very Edwardian-looking gentleman' — this, from Louis Dudek, nicely sums up the sophistication in that face: the face of aplomb, of a man who knows his worth.

Glassco — Buffy, to friends — was at the height of his prestige not only as a poet (*Selected Poems* would go on to win the Governor General's Award for Poetry) but also as a diversely gifted man of letters. *Memoirs of Montparnasse*, a sparkling evocation of expatriate Paris during the 1920s, had been published to wide acclaim the previous year. *The New York Times Book Review* called it 'a delightful, on-the-spot report of the days when it was still possible to be very young, very hip and very happy.' It was joined by *The Poetry of French Canada in Translation*, a landmark anthology in which nearly half the contributions were done by his own hand. Adding to these achievements were critical essays, book reviews, short stories, even pornographic novels. ('We never knew,' Robin Skelton later recalled, 'what he would write next, what he would renew by translation, what he would say.') A first-rate stylist, Glassco deemed writing a challenge best overcome by panache. No matter the genre, he was always garbed in a well-cut form. He ran with a pack of Montreal poets, among them A.J.M. Smith, F.R. Scott and Ralph Gustafson, who brought something courtly and dashing to Canadian letters. Together this 'Montreal Group' embodied a set of ideals — in Glassco's own words: 'mastery of line, cadence, perfection of ear' — that were, in their day, the epitome of cool. And, as the photo proves, even in a group with a well-known punctilio for jackets and ties, Glassco stood apart.

Yet his gaze gives pause. Lidded eyes sit on heavy bags, drained and disillusioned. It reminds us that, besides the suave Glassco readers know (made famous by all the merrymaking and skirt-chasing in *Memoirs*), there's another rarely talked about — the self-loather, the lamenter, the loner. The Glassco who, in a late letter, counted himself among 'the tired generation, the finished men'. The Glassco who, according to biographer Brian Busby, dreaded three things: 'His birthday, Christmas and New Year's Eve.' The Glassco who critic Philip Lanthier claims was 'wracked by the terrors of having lost his way in life'. As it happens, this fellow is fairly easy to find: his poems give him away.

Glassco was one of the first Canadian poets to show a sincere interest in decay. Decades of residence in Quebec's relic-strewn Eastern Townships sharpened his eye for emblems of decline: dilapidated farmhouses, barns, sheds. His tendency to dote on debris, often emphasizing its grungier aspects like 'mouldering walls' or 'tarpaper hanging in tatters', was sometimes seen as evidence of a bathetic bent. (In a 1964 letter, Al Purdy warned Glassco about the risks of swooning over 'ruined things'.) Yet Glassco's poems contrast sharply with the soft-headed rusticity that afflicted Canadian poets at the time, including his Montreal Group. 'It snows on this place,' goes one of Gustafson's typically tranquil lines, 'And a gentleness obtains.' Glassco saw nothing gentle about it. The pastoral, for him, was a postmortem on its own prettiness. Nature spawned weeds, scarecrows, cow-piss puddles, concrete cubes, barbed wire and 'graveyards minding their own business'. Weather was hostile ('sun and rain / Score harshly') and countrysides teemed with malign verbs: choke, crumble, drag, dump, grind, rut, scour, spew. To Northrop Frye, who believed the Canadian imagination was at its best when pitted against 'a huge, unthinking, menacing, and formidable setting', Glassco's reply was: don't bother. Our defeat is a *fait accompli*.

Glassco was acutely aware of his rubble-gawking ('Why do I love you, ragged things?'), and, in some of his best poems, tries to probe it. 'The Burden of Junk', which appeared in his first book, *The Deficit Made Flesh* (1958), finds the poet dropping by a scrap dealer named Corby and his 'Yardful of rusty and broken machinery'. Corby's delight over a recent acquisition—'Swapped the old three-teated cow for a genuine walnut harmonium!'—causes Glassco to reflect on what he can offer in 'trade':

> Mine is a burden of lumber that ought to be left with him also:
> This is where it belongs, with the wheels and the beds and the organ,
> With all the personal trash that the spirit acquires and abandons

Nothing quite like this exists in Canadian poetry before Glassco. Even Atwood's most twisted psychodramas at the height of her 'survivalist' stage fall short of a forty-eight-year-old man comparing himself to a 'burden of lumber' fit to be tossed on a rubbish heap. Glassco's sense of unsuitability was, in part, linked to worries about wasted literary effort. As poets often do, Glassco brooded on his career until fear of neglect mixed indistinguishably with fear of death. This comes into ironic play in the above lines, which grapple with the idea of oblivion in dactylic hexameter (a staple of epic poetry). The lines are also a warning that Glassco's well-groomed bon vivantism can only take us so far when assessing poems one critic called 'splinters from a damaged sensibility'.

'The Burden of Junk' was a breakthrough. Compared to poems by his contemporaries, it carried a different, more mordant, slightly unhealthier idea of what a person was, or could be. Eating away at Glassco was the hard-to-shake sense of being damaged goods. Some of his peers thought Glassco's gift for staging desolate tableaux owed something to the *fin-de-siècle* Decadents. In the passing years, however, poems like 'The Burden of Junk' have revealed themselves to be stranger, more disturbed, more genuine. Far from striking a pose, Glassco feels the unease within his own skin. His best poems are an account of how things — including humans — fall apart. The world for him comes alive only from the bottom down; and even then, only to the extent to which it carries the clarity of its ruin. We can see this in the excellent ending to 'The Burden of Junk'. Fusing earnestness and unsentimentality, the poem draws on memories of Glassco's salad days to evoke 'the loves that a dreary process of dumping / Leaves at last on a hillside to rot away with the seasons.' The slippery ambiguity released by that closing line break, making 'leaves' both noun and verb, both deed and symbol, masterfully embodies Glassco's dead 'loves'. The effect puts 'The Burden of Junk' within shouting distance of other works that explore the impact of discarded matter on identity: Wallace Stevens's 'The Man on the Dump', A.R. Ammons's book-length poem *Garbage* and even Don DeLillo's novel *Underworld*.

Glassco was saddled with the Midas curse: the compulsion to transform pain into art. He was a dab hand at sonnets and could turn a rhyme on a dime. He also had a taste for syntactically daring stanzaic experiments ('Gentleman's Farm' is a three-page poem constructed out of three long sentences). Into these Fabergé forms, he poured acid. An inveterate phrase-jeweller, Glassco was extraordinarily deft at conveying varieties of hard luck: missed chance and failed opportunity, rural lives reduced to 'rotten fenceposts and old mortgages'.

The result, in poem after poem, is a music unfazed by its bleak content. Alternately, you might say Glassco turned gloom into ear candy. Few poets possessed of so much anti-charm have worked harder to win over readers. He gives us striking images of entrapment ('watch the struggles soft moths make / Fast bound within the spider's web'), entombment ('the closed / enclosing house') and decomposition ('papery corpses crumbling'). With their excellent table manners, Glassco's poems mount their upmarket appeal on the illusion of speaking for Wordsworthian nostalgia ('You natural scenes to whose eternity / My transient vision and my life are bound, / Teach me to see'). But searing through his sparkling stanzas and rhymes is something darker: despair at the futility of human life, at how man 'is destined for slaughter in the course of things'. And because Glassco had no goal above that of writing well, it is despair on display, despair that seeks to seduce, with violent images wrapped in plush tones:

> I am a homestead in a hundred acres:
> I draw them around me and devour them.
> I eat the farmer's flesh and his children
> —Who but I hollaed the sweating team?—
> Their hands were worn away in my service,
> Sold my acres one by one to strangers.
> Ere I was done the dying farmer cursed me,
> Crying within the strangling noose of hope.
> I am the grave of the husbandman's hope.

These lines, from 'The White Mansion', are spoken by a century-old house that boasts of using her feminine wiles to ensnare unsuspecting proprietors and drive them to the point of obsession, exhaustion and ruin. The house becomes an avatar for the universe's mean streak, its utter hostility to human happiness: 'I am the death of man and of his dream.' Glassco based his poem on the spacious, manor-like home he moved into in 1936, located on a farm on the outskirts of Knowlton, Quebec. He lived there for over a decade, enjoying an idyllic, semi-reclusive country existence until woman troubles turned the place into a living hell. With its filigreed English, disquieting images ('Grey hills behind me, black water at my feet') and careful application of theatricality to conjure an atmosphere of Gothic noir, the poem is a ravishing demonstration of Glassco's biases. He seemed ready to use any pretext — and every bell and whistle in his literary tool kit — to indulge his appetite for doom.

Biography played a part in this as well. The grim phantasmagoria of Glassco's poetry had roots in an astonishingly brutal upbringing. Glassco, as he revealed in 'Autobiographical Sketch', was raised by a 'sadist' father who beat him savagely during his childhood, a humiliation that triggered years of 'cruel and unremitting nightmares' (the outlines of their relationship can be seen in 'The Whole Hog'.) In this sense, Glassco's taste for the macabre was bred in the bone. It seems fitting therefore that Glassco used masks ('masks that misery has put on') to vent his feelings. Aside from the pseudonyms adopted for his erotic novels, Glassco also turned to historical figures whose lives, he felt, held moments of crisis that mirrored his own. These include medieval religious writer Thomas à Kempis, and the half-mad French painter Utrillo. Translation afforded yet another mask. He found his greatest affinity with Quebecois poet Saint-Denys Garneau, whose anguish-ridden journals and poems ('Oh into what wilderness we must go / To die quietly by ourselves') moved him deeply.

By these repeated bifurcations, Glassco not only assembled a Greek chorus of doppelgangers, but also revealed a key truth about himself: his civilized tendencies were the reverse side of a horrified self-knowledge, one too hot to handle directly. His disguises freed him to speak. His most memorable alter-ego in this regard was iconic fashion plate Beau Brummel. Nineteenth-century 'it' boy and the inventor of dandyism, Brummel, who was celebrated for his razor wit and sense of style, died in an asylum, penniless and syphilitic. One of Glassco's finest and most revealing poems, 'Brummell at Calais' is a portrait of 'a foolish useless man' done in by narcissism and whom posterity further punishes by remembering him precisely for his superficiality. The poem ends on what Glassco calls 'The triumph of his veritable art':

> An art of being, nothing but being, the grace
> Of perfect self-assertion based on nothing,
> As in our vanity's cause against the void
> He strikes his elegant blow, the solemn report of those
> Who have done nothing and will never die.

Those familiar with Glassco's chronic doubts about himself ('I have turned out a failure in everything I have tried to do,' he wrote in an early letter) may find it hard to read these lines as anything other than a stinging self-indictment. Glassco, after all, was Canada's dandy-poet, the literary arbiter elegantiarum of his day. It was a role he publicly relished (George Fetherling tells a story of paying Glassco an early morning visit and finding him already in a silk smoking jacket and cravat, sipping breakfast champagne). But if his author photograph is any hint, fears he had fallen prey to Brummellian vanity were maybe starting to take hold. What Glassco's face betrays, in other words, is a poet coming to terms with the possibility of his own ridiculousness.

Something of a slow starter, Glassco didn't publish his first book, *The Deficit Made Flesh*, until he was nearly fifty. He assembled poems with a deep pleasure in their constructedness (he once defined good poems as having 'a beginning, a middle and an end'). The pleasure wasn't unwarranted. Metrical fluency was still, in many circles, the *ne-plus-ultra*. True, those circles were rapidly shrinking, but rhyme and meter remained part of the larger frame of reference. It was a period that welcomed experiments (see Earle Birney's typographically wild 'Appeal to a Lady With a Diaper') but didn't relieve poets of the duty to satisfy expectations of form and meaning. It was a period that hankered after thrilling oddness (see Avison's jaggedly energetic 'The Butterfly') but stayed loyal to poetry as beautiful language. Alas, ideas of good poetry, and the reputations they buoy, are always vulnerable to changes in taste — trend shifts that can drain those ideas of their authority and leave careers high and dry.

Which is exactly what happened. By the time Glassco's photo

was snapped, the larky, natty youth had become, in his own words, 'a newmade ghost'. We can read it plainly on his face. In newspaper profiles he could still play the 'elegantly tailored' cad who spent his afternoons 'thinking, reading, and fortifying himself with martinis'. But the anachronism of the role had been remorselessly exposed by an emerging generation that targeted him in their political-cultural dissent. 'All of John Glassco's works,' wrote the thirty-four-year-old poet-critic Frank Davey in 1974, 'have been eccentric achievements, more attached to the values and fashions of the past than to those of post-war Canada.' The reason Davey could write such a sentence, and feel confident doing so, was because the national aesthetic had shifted from the mid-Atlantic voice (Anglo-American in diction, Canadian in content) popularized by the Montreal Group. Thanks in large part to *TISH*, Vancouver became the new beachhead. Founded in 1961 as a poetry newsletter (its name is an anagram of 'shit'), it regarded itself as a reset button on Canadian poetry's colonial hang-up. It was *TISH*, of which Davey was a founding member, that first raised alarms about the 'Eurocentrism' of poets like Glassco. A cocktail of countercultural fed-up-ness, mud-slinging, and political anxieties, *TISH* successfully tapped into a rising exhaustion with high culture. Anything too revised or technically confident, anything that chimed and rhymed, was square. Or worse, frivolous: cocooned inside an anti-world of style.

In such an environment, a poet like Glassco was easy to mock. In his review of Glassco's second book, *A Point of Sky* (1964), bill bissett was characteristically scathing: 'They all look like bad trips to me.' Those sorts of hipster sentences—*TISH* had a gift for trash talk—did mortal damage to Glassco's reputation. At first, he pushed back. In one poem, he dismissed the *TISH*-leaning poems popping up in magazines as 'poetics about poetics about poetics'. He also took a stab at a spoof sound poem, a lark called 'A Catbird' (representative line: 'k'tuf à tuf à tuf à tuf à tuf à te kerry'). But it did no good. The more successfully *TISH* practised its dark arts, the funnier Glassco's ascots and dinner jackets looked. Until he himself was moved to write in a journal in the early seventies: 'I have been rejected as a serious writer, and acclaimed as a clown.'

As is often the case in these generational skirmishes, a real weakness in Canadian poetry was being exposed. *TISH* wanted nothing to do with the 'culture-objects' flooding the domestic market, produced by Eastern Canadian poets for whom form was, in Davey's words, a 'showplace for the human mind'. And who could blame them? Many of the formalist tics that drove *TISH* crazy can certainly be spotted in Glassco: too-pretty gratuitousness, too-ponderous wordplay, a grapple with language that doesn't know when to let go. Glassco's trouble is that he absorbed, but never came to distrust, the classic cadences of English poetry. 'Later poets learn their craft from earlier,' writes critic William Logan, 'but they must provide the originality themselves, in resistance to what they learn.' So when Glassco's poems fail, they fail not from a negligent handling of his devices, but from a too-confident embrace of them. They fail for being all too aware of how it's supposed to be done.

Such an assessment, no doubt, squares up with what readers may already surmise about the period. And that's because — as is also often the case in these generational skirmishes — history is written by the victors. It can be a surprise, then, to find poems by Glassco that burn with self-assurance, emotional resonance, many-rooted wordplays and memorable speech. These traits also exemplify everything that, for a period, allowed a phalanx of mid-century Montreal poets to dominate the skyline. Poets like Smith, Scott, Leo Kennedy and A.M. Klein introduced a dizzying range of new effects into Canadian poetry, from the colloquially offhand to the tightly epigrammatic. Together they strived to create an audience for world-class poetry that put a premium on intellectual idiosyncrasy, was technically mettlesome and brandished an exacting sense of diction. All of these ideas were plowed into the production of exemplary and enduring poems, some of which rank among the glories of Canadian poetry: Scott's 'Lakeshore', Klein's 'Portrait of the Poet as Landscape', Gustafson's 'The Newspaper' and Glassco's 'Gentleman's Farm'.

For *TISH*, these poets were CanPo's 'burden of lumber'. Their writing as outlandish as anything in Palgrave's nineteenth-century anthology *The Golden Treasury*. Glassco, beaten down, began paying attention. Maybe he felt they had a point, maybe he wanted to show he wasn't stuck in his ways or maybe the avant-garde winds just threw him. Whatever it was, two years after he published his *Selected Poems*, Glassco went on to self-publish his last, and oddest, book of poetry, *Montreal* (1973). An 'epic-macaronic' whistle-stop tour of his memories of Montreal, the poem turned its streets to metaphoric rubble, an ugly no man's land. The city was now a place full of old stuff. The voice is held together by interspersings of French sentences and Indigenous references embedded in sprawling, theatrical, ample stanzas that swing between free verse and rhyme. It's a portrait of the fogey as loser, blackballed by fate, the odd man out. The whole thing has the feel of a panic attack:

> All furious frustrated honkings, I fly like a wild goose
> Over all your hallowed ground, O Montreal,
> Annihilating Jeanne and Maisonneuve
> Dorchester and Saint-Denis
> McTavish and McGill,
> Crushing my memories of your streets, passing
> Into another world, moving
> Into another country of the anarchic mind

With its sophisticated notes mingled with maladroit moments, *Montreal* seemed to embody for Glassco a genuine confusion about how to continue writing poems (one critic called it 'half-cocked', another critic said it had 'the shock value of the worst *TISH* poetry'). Canadian poetry would, of course, go on to do different things, things Glassco could scarcely have imagined. And one can't help but feel in this poem that the shape of that future — our reality — had started to download some of its own confusion into his life.

For all the pleasure principles he represented — technical giftedness, unimpeachable wordplay — Glassco is the saddest of all Canadian poets. He forged a fatalism that, poised between vigour and elegance, was new to us. You came for the style, but stayed for the woe. When he passed away in 1981, so too did the most cavalier heyday of Canadian poetry, a circle now under deep anti-formalist suspicion, effectively given the heave-ho. To borrow John Bayley's example of Wordsworth, they are 'like one's parents' clothes — always out of fashion'. But surely one of the great tasks of twenty-first-century critics will be to help us think again about these figures, among whom Glassco stands tall.

The Rural Mail

These are the green paths trodden by patience.
I hang on the valley's lip, a bird's eye viewing
All that opposes to makers and masters of nations
Only its fierce mistrust of the word —
To the smashed records for gobbling and spewing,
Cows that exist in a slow-motion world.

For here is man on man's estate of nature,
Farmer on farm, the savage civilized
Into the image of his God the weather —
Only another anarchist, foiled highflyer
Whose years have grown as a minute in his eyes,
Whose grin reveals a vision of barbed wire:

Here birth evokes pleasure and a reflective pity,
Marriage or mating, much of the voyeur,
Sickness, an interest and some hope of booty,
And death strikes like an oddly barked command,
Confounding with its *Easy*, its *As you were*,
His stiff-kneed generation unused to bend.

I sense his hours marked by my two-wheeled cart
Descending the stony hill: as I stop by his box
The ring of tin as the *Knowlton News* goes in
Is a days' knell — and the countryside contracts
For an instant to the head of a pin;
Or he comes with a money-order, or to chat.

Getting good money, and money is always good,
We keep the high standards in the front parlour
Like a wedding-cake or a motto carved in wood,
The falling-out of enemies makes no friends.
'Far as I'm concerned, the war can go on forever!'
A man can *make* a dollar, with hens.

Scraping the crumbling roadbed of this strife
With rotten fenceposts and old mortgages
(No way of living, but a mode of life),
Now sift from death and waste three grains of duty,
O thoughts that start from scratch and end in a dream
Of graveyards minding their own business?

But the heart accepts it all, this honest air
Lapped in green valleys where accidents will happen!
Where the bull, the buzz-saw and the balky bare
Are the chosen fingers of God for a farmer's sins,
Like the axe for his woods, and his calves and chicks and children
Destined for slaughter in the course of things.

Stud Groom

Your boy's-ambition was to be a Horseman,
Some day to hear tell or overhear your name
Linked with that word. This was the foreseen
Reward for the five years in the dealer's stable,
For strewing your childhood nightly under his horses' feet
And bearing it out at sun-up on a shovel,

When you met all claims with waiver and deferment,
And learned the habit of not coming to grips
With any unhaltered thing that's not dependent
On a boy's will like a pious man on God's,
Till language lapsed back into clucks and chirps,
Hisses and heeyahs, steady-babes, be-goods.

And now it has all come true! and the mountains spill
Your world of cousins, a chorus of witnesses:
Lost Nation, Bolton Centre and Pigeon Hill
Acclaim you who combine, deny and defer
With straps and stalls the heats and the rampancies,
And the act that's blessed with a bucket of cold water.

Well, there is the World, in the attitude of approval,
Hands in its pockets, hat over its eyes,
Ignorant, cunning, suave and noncommittal,
The ape of knowledge.... Say, through what injustice
Has it gained the bounty, by what crazy process
Those eyes fell heir to your vision of success?

For the goal has changed.—It's rather to have made
Of the welcoming music of knickers and whinnies
At feeding time, the brightness of an eye
Fixed on a bucket, the fine restraint of a hoof
Raised and held in a poised meaningless menace,
To have made, of these, assurances of love,

And of the denial of all loving contact
When the ears flatten, the eye rolls white,
The whirring alarm that keeps the dream intact
For poet and pervert too, whose spasm or nightmare
Makes, with the same clean decision of a bite,
Divorce between possession and desire.

For 'one woman leads to another, like one war
Leads to another,' and the fever has no end
Till passion turns — from the bright or bloody star,
From the bitter triumph over a stranger's body,
To something between a deity and a friend,
To a service halting between cult and hobby,

And nothing is left for the family or the nation
But a genial curse, and silence. It may be
You are the type of figures long out of fashion,
The Unknown Soldier and the Forgotten Man,
Whom the rest might envy now, their anonymity
And the fact they were at least left alone;

And who might have said, like you, to a pair
Of nags looking over a sagging roadside fence,
Good Morning, girls! O greeting washed in air,
O simple insistence to affirm the Horse,
While the Loans and bomb-loads are hitting new highs
And youth is deducted at the source.

For 'Horseman, what of the future?' is a question
Without a meaning: there is always another race,
Another show, the unquenchable expectation
Of ribbons, the easy applause like a summer storm,
And the trill, like love, of being in first place
For an instance that lasts forever, and does no harm

Except to the altar-fated passion it robs,
The children it cheats of their uniforms and wars,
And the fathomless future of the underdog
It negates — shrugs off like the fate of a foundered mare —
As it sparks the impenetrable lives, like yours
Whose year revolves around the country fair.

The Entailed Farm

A footpath would have been enough.
The muddy mile of side-road has no purpose
Save as it serves for others to link up
Crossroads marked on the map with a nameless cross
By way of these choked and heartless fields of paintbrush
And the mute, sealed house,

Where the spring's tooth, stripping shingles, scaling
Beam and clapboard, probes for the rot below
Porch and pediment and blind bow-window,
And the wooden trunk with the coloured cardboard lining
Lies where it fell when the wall of the flying wing
Fell down ten years ago;

Where the stone wall is a haven for snake and squirrel,
The steepled dovecote for phoebe and willow-wren,
And the falling field-gates, trigged by an earthen swell,
Open on a wild where nothing is raised or penned,
On rusty acres of witch-grass and wild sorrel
Where the field-birds cry and contend.

You, tourist, salesman, family out for a picnic,
Who saw the bearded man that walked like a bear,
His pair of water-pails slung from a wooden neckyoke,
Slipping in by the woodshed—Come away,
That naked door is proof against all knocking!
Standing and knocking there,

You might as well expect time's gate to open
On the living past, the garden bloom again,
The house stand upright, hay-barn's swayback coping
Stiffen, and see as in a fretted frame
Men in the meadow and a small boy whooping
The red oxen down that orchard lane,

Or revive the slow strong greed of the coffined farmer
Who cleared, stumped, fenced, rotating sinew and sweat,
Beating the ploughshare into an honest dollar,
Who living and dying planned to cheat time's night
Through the same white-bearded boy — who is hiding somewhere
Now, till you're out of sight,

And have left him alone: alone with the grief or anger
Or whatever it is that flickers but will not die
In the dull brain of the victim turned avenger,
At war with a shadow, in flight from passers-by,
From us — who are free from all but the hint of attainder,
Who can meet a stranger's eye

With a good face, can answer a question, give a reason,
For whom the world's fields and fences stand up plain,
Nor dazzle in sunlight or crumble behind the rain:
From us, with our hearts but lightly tinged with poison,
Who composed our quarrel early and in good season
Buried the hatchet in our father's brain.

Gentleman's Farm

Ten miles from anywhere eighty years and more,
Where the frozen roadstones grind iron shoes and tires
And the timberwood's last stand
Lives only in brushwood and long memories — see,
The new-peeled posts are marching, the taut wires
Sing to the naked land,

Sing to the valley of slash and beaver-meadow,
The stone-pocked fields and bog-born stunted alders
And the black hills rising sheer
As mountains of iron and sand round the Genie's castle
(The age-old view of eyes that each November
Look back on a wasted year),

That things are humming, that even here at last
The lights are going on, the wheels going round
As the wasteland fulfils
The singular purpose, powered and glorified
Of the weekday absentee whose will has broken
Between these barren hills,

And where the regional serf, time out of mind,
Morning and evening, blind with sweat and fury,
Hollaed his shaggy tyke
After the peaked-arse cows in the hummocky pasture
Till they buckjumped to the dislocated barn,
Their slack bags black with muck,

The silos rise and the cupolas of chrome,
Minarets of the mosque, the milkwhite temple
Gleaming below the hill —
And look, by the mailbox winks the coloured legend,
Hillsview Farm, the Home of Reg'd Holsteins
Stamped on a plaque of steel.

What passion is this? What fancy fed with tractors,
Engines and rancho-fence and palisades?
        Not here, at least,
Has the urban dream flowered in a homing impulse
Towards the inane, imagined verities
        In the soil, the dung, the teats —

Things of an island whose longed-after earth
The city of Columbus, falling on his knees,
        Kisses and calls it Saviour,
Making his garden where he can, his plea
Against the unreal tenures which enrage
        A street-begotten fever —

No, this is a dream-barn, a body of wood and iron
Figuring forth on the mind's wilderness,
        With wealth for an ally,
The structural mania of the human heart —
Whose buildings rise in a kinder soil than this,
        And beneath an inward eye

Where all goes well and the pioneer has profit,
Where the titan's work subserves as in a dream
        The all too fictive goal,
And the end is perfect beauty, the blessed vision,
The working out of a man's reverie
        Of his own memorial!

But here, while the eternal mountains stand,
Immortal stones come up beneath the plough,
        This valley's sun and rain
Score harshly and the bitten autumnal crop,
Scratched out with a hoe or shovelled by machines,
        Is still the same:

O forefixed harvest of man's reverie driven
Into the light of day and life of men,
    You bring the same revenge
On the impresarios of all sacred sweetness,
Whose eyes shall wake to witness, spring by spring,
    The sad and stealing change,

Hope battered into habit, and a habit
Running to weariness — the proof and process
    Of powers which must equate
Farmer and Gentleman through their monuments,
Till time's mathematic of indifference
    Confound them, to create

Not the bare living nor the orgulous legend
(Improbable flowers from seed of sweat or treasure),
    But what's more tenuous still,
A feast for the idler and the ragamuffin,
A more conspicuous waste of all endeavour
    That has had its will —

A common loveliness! — Look backward now,
As we breast the rubbly hill to the rotting sawmill,
    Back to the shining roof
That parries the pale far flung November sunlight
On lightning rods and a stammering weathervane
    Of a gilded calf:

See that the wreck of all things made with hands
Being fixed and certain, as all flesh is grass,
    The grandiose design
Must marry the ragged thing, and of the vision
Nothing endure that does not gain through ruin
    The right, the wavering line.

Deserted Buildings Under Shefford Mountain

These native angels of decay
        In shed and barn whose broken wings
Lie here half fallen in the way
Of headstones amid uncut hay—
        Why do I love you, ragged things?

What grace unknown to any art,
        What beauty frailer than a mood
Awake in me their counterpart?
What correspondence of a heart
        That loves the failing attitude?

Here where I grasp the certain fate
        Of all man's work in wood and stone,
And con the lesson of the straight
That shall be crooked soon or late
        And crumble into forms alone,

Some troubled joy that's half despair
        Ascends within me like a breath:
I see these silent ruins where
The speaking look, the sleeping air
        Of features newly cast in death,

Dead faces where we strive to see
        The signature of something tossed
Between design and destiny,
Between God and absurdity,
        Till, harrowing up a new-made ghost,

We half embrace the wavering form,
        And half conceive the wandering sense
Of some imagined part kept warm
And salvaged from the passing storm
        Of time's insulting accidents.

So I, assailed by the blind love
    That meets me in this silent place,
Lift open arms: Is it enough
That restless things can cease to move
    And leave a ruin wreathed in grace,

Or is this wreck of strut and span
    No more than solace for the creed
Of progress and its emmet plan,
Dark houses that are void of man,
    Dull meadows that have gone to seed?

The White Mansion

I am a bright thing on my rising ground,
A green hill behind me, a blue brook at my feet.
The dawn reddens my eastern doors,
The whirling sun makes my windows a glory.
The woods around me a hundred years ago
Were felled to raise my naked arms.
Ere I was done the hairy pioneer
Fell dead exulting in his dream.
I am the death of man and of his dream.

I am a homestead in a hundred acres:
I draw them around me and devour them.
I eat the farmer's flesh and his children
— Who but I hollaed the sweating team? —
Their hands were worn away in my service,
Sold my acres one by one to strangers.
Ere I was done the dying farmer cursed me,
Crying within the strangling noose of hope.
I am the grave of the husbandman's hope.

I am a shining temple, a tall man's pride.
My groves are planted with plumy pines.
Through my avenues of cedar, my stone pillars,
Fly slender horses, tracery of wheels.
My lights were seen all through the summer night.
Within and without, he dressed me in splendour.
Ere I was done, I stripped him naked,
Sent him away weeping, to beg for money.
I am the dancer blown with tears and money.

I am the fairest court of love and pleasure.
My hedges tangle, my lawn return to hay;
The woods crept up to my rotted door-sills,
Stones fell in, but ever amid the mouldering walls
The holy fire streamed upright on the altar:
Two hearts, two bodies clove, knew nothing more.
Ere I was done, I tore them asunder. Singly
They fled my ruin and the ruin of love.
I am she who is stronger than love.

I shall never be done: no man shall see it.
My brightness overtops his dream.
I am the scourge of hope: I bury my servants.
I am the sink of wealth: behold my trees.
I am the tomb of love: the altar is broken.
Swan-white I float among bare crusted maples.
Grey hills behind me, black water at my feet,
I await the stroke from which I shall arise
To announce once more the death of man.

The Brill Road

Skeletons of scarecrows, buoys for the sailor of snow,
The broomhead sticks of brush tell where it goes
Straight into a white screaming sky
Of tons of a snowblind wind scouring like sand
The walls of the last valley-house in the half-light,
Where its lap would be if the mountain were a man.

And the mare looks back: are we going upwards, master?
Yes, we follow the blinding years,
Into the sweeping, swallowing wind,
Into the gape of all and the loss of the person
Driving his birthright deathward in a trance
Over the mountain's swollen Jovian brow,

Like a mind grappling with its own betrayal,
Thoughts thinning out, the basis crumbling,
Rising, rising ever into more breathless air
And a frailer tenure, while the wind blows,
The hills darken, and this heaven-writing road thrown
Like a noosed lifeline to five worthless farms
Peters out under the snow.

The road is a trick, like every form of life,
A signal into the dark impartial storm
(The leveller of land, the old mount-maker
Smoother of great and small): though the road is wrong
Always, and leads upwards forever
To impossible heights, into the boiling snow,
There is no turning back; but the road is a trap.

This is the involvement that we never sought.
How should we know its conditions, terms
Determined by the swollen alien brow?
Only we do the mountain's bidding, while the storm
Beats in our eyes, exhausts our servants,
Tearing the robe from knee and shoulder,
Making a terrible half-light of our day.

And from this day we drive into the trap,
Seeking the mountain, the five worthless farms.
Do we move to a screaming music, is that all?
What is this orchestra of fear? Absurd
Are the equations for us and our servants
Madly seeking the other side of the mountain.
Does it even exist, that quiet road
Snow-pleached between the laden, bending trees
Where the small, fat birds will be flitting and feeding,
Where the wind is muffled and we move at peace?

The Burden of Junk

April again, and its message unvaried, the same old impromptu
Dinned in our ears by the tireless dispassionate chortling of Nature,
Sunlight on grey land, the grey of the past like a landscape around us
Caught in its moment of nakedness also, a pitiful prospect
Bared to the cognitive cruelty shining upon it: O season,
Season that leads me again, like this road going over the mountain,
Past the old landmarks and ruins, the holdfasts of hope and ambition—

Why is the light doubly hard on the desolate places? why even
Hardest of all on the tumbledown cabin of Corby the Trader?
See, with its tarpaper hanging in tatters, the doorstep awash in a
Puddle of cow-piss and kindling-chips, ringed with the mud of a fenceless
Yardful of rusty and broken machinery, washstands and bedsteads,
Bodies of buggies and berlots, the back seats of autos, bundles of
Chicken-wire, leaves of old wagon-springs and miscellaneous
        wheels.... But

There is Corby himself in the mud and the sunshine, in front of the
Lean-to cowshed, examining something that looks like a sideboard,
Bidding me stop and admire, and possibly make him an offer:
'Swapped the old three-teated cow for a genuine walnut harmonium!
Look, ain't a scratch or a brack in it anywhere—pedals and stopples
Work just as good as a fellow could ask for! Over to Broome they
Say they used to cost four hundred dollars apiece from the factory....'

Here is the happy collector of objects, the absolute type of
All who engage in the business of buying and shifting, the man who
Turns a putative profit into an immediate pleasure,
Simply by adding a zero to his account with a self-owned
Bank of Junk, and creates a beautiful mood of achievement
Out of nothing at all! Ah here is the lord of the cipher,
This is the Man of the Springtime, the avatar of Lyaeus!

We should be trading indeed, if we could, I think as I leave him.
Mine is a burden of lumber that ought to be left with him also:
This is where it belongs, with the wheels and the beds and the organ,
With all the personal trash that the spirit acquires and abandons,
Things that have made the heart warm and bewildered the senses with
beauty
Long ago — but that weakened and crumbled away with the passion
Born of their brightness, the loves that a dreary process of dumping
Leaves at last on a hillside to rot away with the seasons.

The Art of Memory

But is it so, as one remembers Carthage
who has seen it? No.
—St Augustine, *Confessions*, x, 19

To be awake today is to be warned.
The unwrinkled lake, the landscape and the leaves
Shimmered all morning, sails and yellow flowers
Dragging another glory from the dead.

The sun of noon, annunciator, struck:
An hour returning from another world.
Blink! go the eyes, in the middle of it all,
Wanting Athene's shield of glassy brass;

Wanting the paradisal past's intenser light,
My eyelids burn: this hour's page
Is a blur of words, and every word in flames.... Oh then
Alas for all familiar things and thoughts,
For the clear of vanished presences before me,

And for their meaning to me, here and now,
As only pegs and props, characters
In the fable of a being—oh infinitely
Remote: I mean, daffodils in a vase,
Sail on the water, sunlight on the grass.

So if no more, why then no more. The train
Of images romance drew in her wake
Like stars in water, troubled and yet true,
Those floating points that charmed a universe

To an idea of itself not wholly
Base, and impressed their fictions here and there—
Shine, fictions that are feelings, shine forever
In the blue aspect of Armance's eyes!

Sift now and handle that too-sacred dust,
And be its fool again, daring the holy deeps,
Having ado with desire, the dark stranger,
Playing with gods, the faces upon coins,

But all in game — the stake, as it was between
That pair of royal apes that ribbed Gonzalo,
A laughter, a waking-up! Till you too wake
And hear time itself talking:

'I am this day, this hour, that speaks: mine is
The smooth-tongued challenge of time saying,
I give you this hour, perfect, splendid, shining,
Spill it before you. Here it is at last:

Here is the empty frame, the gilded stage
Set for high deeds, adoration, what you will,
For happiness deferred, guarded so long:
I do my part. I show my hand. Take the key.'

And here is the dry light, the beach of stones.
Never will earth break open or god speak,
No Curtius mount and gallop
Full-armed into the public pit —

Only eyes closing, hooded from the sun,
Suffice in this splenetic hour to ease
The lust of matter, flagrat of dry bones
Sluiced with the humours of an afternoon,

When how to accept the blank of closing doors,
As saints and martyrs do their palms and pains,
Is the only question: to retrieve in desperation
What was rejected in despite: to see

Items as undiscoverable isles
And leave them so, with the accidental ocean
Laving their lambent whatness — to the sense
Inviolate, beyond geography,

And so much deeper by so far untouched
By hope or hunger. So I do, I do;
So leave them as they were, poised on the point
Of what they are this moment, and so resign
The flowers to yellow and the lake to blue.

The Whole Hog

When I was very young my mother told me
That my father was the strongest of men
(Not in words at first, of course—but I knew);
Later I learned he was the best and bravest;
And during my adolescence (a difficult
Time for us all) I had her whispered word for it
He was the wisest parent in the world.

Long ago I put aside the question
Of her motive in this matter.... Perhaps
A sense of guilt for the disloyalty
Of a too-clear, too-wifely-valuation
Of his man's-worth, was expiated so:
Enough that I too now appreciate
The situation, and appraise the need.

For now I wonder about his part only,
Asking myself through just what consciousness
Of his own fragility the man was induced
To accept this grand vocation—as he did —
And dropping all else, set himself to become
Great God to a little child? It is a question
That opens up vistas of personal hell....

To be the Absolute to someone else:
Figure the concitations of the demon
That drove him to this! Like a hunted beast,
Like a starving man, like a falling stone,
He followed his blind will to its end in nature,
Projected himself into infinity
And silvered a looking-glass in his son's eye.

I try to guess what image haunted him,
What spectral littleness of man alone:
Paltry Invictus with the head of clay
Jabbered at him from the pools in his mind,
Loomed in the coalsacks of its sky, met him
At flowery turnings in his private garden,
In sleep, in love, at billiards, at the ball;

Until he must have realized that the world was
Not only too much with him, but too much for him—
For poor Invictus, the poor gentleman
Who laid claim, simply, to the whole universe,
But brought no vouchers, bore no strawberry mark!
And when lovely woman failed him, womanly,
He built an altar in the sands of my heart.

I have not sacrificed there for years ...
But the altar stands, eternal absolute,
As if its foundations were laid in living rock;
And when I went whoring after strange gods,
Why, they were Gods, and it was whoring still—
With reason, unreason, duality of will,
And many others, masks of Nobodaddy,

In my father's house there were no dissensions,
There, all was unanimity and family:
Now the plates fly in my head night and day;
There, was infallible authority:
Now I am free as a crow to fly or stay;
There, was no check nor doubt nor indecision:
Here I am a dog whistled by many masters,

Always obliged to go the whole hog,
And with no hambone even to drop in the water;
Nosing about the world for love and tid-bits
I am still baffled by the faith-breakings
Of flesh in season and sonorous language
That tell me I also am a piece of property
And rouse only my barking rhetoric in answer;

For experience only leads me about in a circle,
And learning by heart still leaves my heart rebellious
To the violent patterns, the makeshift morals
Whose insoluble equation leaves me as cold
As the by-blow baby left all night on the doorstep:
—That home with wealthy windows lit, is mine!

See the Portland vase before the Venetian mirror
In my father's house. It is filled with *honesty*.
The abstraction found its body long ago
In a plant of eternally desiccated leaves,
As my father's demons spoke of his hold forever
On my heart, and mine of the fragile tenure
Of all things: we have learned the porcine betrayals.

Quebec Farmhouse

Admire the face of plastered stone
The roof descending like a song
Over the washed and anointed walls,
Over the house that hugs the earth
Like a feudal souvenir: oh see
The sweet submissive fortress of itself
That the landscape owns!

And inside is the night, the airless dark
Of the race so conquered it has made
Perpetual conquest of itself,
Upon desertion's ruin piling
The inward desert of surrender,
Drawing in all its powers, puffing its soul,
Raising its arms to God.

This is the closed, enclosing house
That set its flinty face against
The rebel children dowered with speech
To break it open, to make it live
And flower in the cathedral beauty
Of a pure heaven of Canadian blue—
The larks so maimed

They still must hark and hurry back
To the paradisal place of gray,
The clash of keys, the click of beads,
The sisters walking leglessly,
While under the wealth and weight of stone
All the bright demons of forbidden joy
Shriek on, year after year.

A House in the Country

The crazy way in which it stands
Proclaims the house was built with hands;
Its gardens so long have wanted care
The flowers now seem intruders where
Priapus and Pomona were;
And both of them must be irate,
So fallen from their former state,
Their shrines broken and desolate,
To see how thistle, burdock, weed,
Flourish, flower and spread their seed.
Like broken furrows run the paths,
The gravel's overgrown with grass,
And half the grass is choked with moss;
The kitchen garden lies outspread
As if all gardeners were dead:
Those hidden, rotting cucumber frames
You'll trip over and break your shins;
This trailing arbour bears a vine
Whose grapes so bitter, bare and thin,
No miracle could turn to wine.

A timid tramp went by last night,
And at the staring sheep took fright:
The poor chilled devil as he ran
Cursed dogs as enemies of man —
And such an incident can please
When barge-lights in the shore-line trees
Are all that break our reveries.

And when the rains come on we'll set
Pans in the attic to catch the drip,
And watch the struggles soft moths make
Fast bound within the spider's web,
Or see the dangling spinner drop
To bind his prey, then kill and sup;
Admire his sturdy consort's knack
Of bearing the babies on her back;
Observe, too, as we see her bite
His head off in an amorous bout,
How love engenders appetite.

We have clean air, meat, cheese and ale
To keep our wits from growing stale,
And the occasional visitor
To remind us what our duties are.

Luce's Notch

Here's where the road ends, on this windy height
Over Bolton Wood, where fifteen years ago
I climbed one summer day, turned round and stopped
Amazed at the beauty of the valleys seen
From the stones of Luce's ruined doorway: then,
I would come back some day, I thought; and so
Turned my back to it and kept climbing on,
Walking beside my two-wheeled cart, while Phyllis
Plodded between the shafts, her chestnut flanks
Wrinkling, straining, her head between her knees,
As the road became a pathway, lost its face
In hummocks, boulders, chattering streams and then
Died in a thin flat meadow fenced with stones,
A place enclosed, where the surrounding slopes
Ran out so far the view was quite cut off;
And at the farther end a rutted gap
Gave on the ruins of a grassy lane,
Which following we at last came out and down
On the road to St. Etienne.

Never again
Did I go that way, and never shall. The road
Is blocked now: see, not only choked with brush
And saplings, but inalterably sealed
By two half-hidden massive concrete cubes
Joined by a length of iron pipe: why not?
Who goes to St. Etienne? Or if he does
Who in his senses ever chose to go
These fifty years by way of Luce's Notch?
However that may be, whatever fool
I was in those days — for I often went
By curious ruined ways and roundabouts —
This is the road's end now, this stop the last;
From here the only way is turning back
To join the links of casual circles leading
Home, or somewhere else I have been before.

—The road is blocked, the chestnut mare is dead,
The cart is mouldering in the loft, and I
Stand here alone, seeing how on this height
That leans over the green gulf of Bolton Glen,
With the intervolved valleys locked in the haze
Of still midsummer, how on this dizzy height
Robin and swallow still fight against the wind
Blown from the mountain whose thin meadows run
Rippling into the sky—stand here again
Beside the wreck of Aaron Luce's barn,
Fronting the valley after fifteen years,
Seeing nothing that I did not see that day,
Feeling only the same despair before things
Still alien, still mysterious, still removed.

There is no outward change: the silvery barn,
All that is left of the work of Luce's hands,
Still stands, tilted at the same angle of falling
It had then (for the buildings hereabouts
Are long in standing, longer still in falling,
And wear for a man's lifetime the final grace
Of tottering and attrition like a crown);
Nothing has changed in all this quiet scene,
And least of all where—not so far above
Eye-level now, across the trough of green —
Old Foster lifts his round and ruined head
Into the sky, a mound of wrinkled stone
Sprinkled with thin white birches.

Ah, but now
Mounted as high as this above the world,
And higher still above all things comprising
The round of living—memories, affections,
The daily tasks and duties, so much of the earth
As binds us to it, inexorably dear!—

Now, if at any time, I should resolve
The secret of that despair, should understand
Why all things radiant and remote in nature —
The fields, the woods, the waterfalls and rocks,
And scenes like this, the valley's green expanse
Seen from the stones of Luce's ruined doorway —
Bring me, as ever, a feeling close to tears.

In earlier days I thought I knew the spring
Of that ecstatic suffering which is joy,
That sense of being unable to possess
A natural scene, or be possessed by it,
That grief engendered by the desperate wish
To make such moments last forever, to stop
Time's hands and the very passage of the blood,
Freeze every conscious faculty, and then —
In a reversal of the course whereby,
As with the loves of saints, desire itself
Is made through the alchemy of their God's grace
The mode of some diviner discontent —
Let all my shapeless flame of yearning change,
Harden and materialize into the form
Of sensual appetite: in those days, indeed,
There seemed one reason only for this pain:
Its end was in its beginning, it was only
In the same rank as the natural affections,
An aspect of inordinate desire.
        This madness I have no more. I only see
Beauty continues, and so do not I.
I have become an ageing eye through which
A young man looks again and trembles, lost
To his own present — and he had no past —
For all his future is what I have become,
A man on a mountain after fifteen years,

A man implicit in that careless heart
Even then when all his idle study was
To drive about the hills in search of strangeness,
Seeking he knew not what, and now has found
Here on this windy height — his wandering loves
Come home to importune him with sorrow now
And fill this foolish ageing child of his
With the sense of what is always failing, fleeting,
Falling away into the gulf of time.
Was it so strong, that careless idle heart?
Do I exist entirely in that man?
A man's identity is never certain,
And least of all my own: today it seems
My whole existence is a pointless dream
Beneath old Foster's blind, tree-sprinkled head;
I am a breath, a nothing, an illusion,
A foolish brain jailed in a creaking skull,
With neither youth nor age, nor any time
To be or to become, so speed the seasons
That waste my substance in these lovely places.
And yet not wholly so; for still I feel
That these green fields, these waterfalls and woods,
These valleys and these winding roads that follow
Always the heights — no matter at what length,
Time being nothing to the men who made them! —
That all these things which now are quite confused
In a beautiful composite of man and nature,
So that even old Foster seems to bless
The farms spread out beneath his weightless shadow,
That they, who are made to outlast my span of vision,
And in whose life the glimpses that I gain
Of the mute, breathing beauty of the world
Stand as a passing moment only, a blink
Between me and the everlasting darkness,
May come to consciousness through me.

Therefore,

You natural scenes to whose eternity
My transient vision and my life are bound,
Teach me to see: give me eyes all over
To multiply the adoration that is in me
For all your insensate parts, for every stone,
For every little watercourse that runs
Between its alders and forget-me-nots,
Daisy and wild rose; keep me as I am now,
Here on this solitary mountain-top,
Purged of each last impulsion of desire
To make you mine, to carry you along
On the wings of possession! Let me be:
Release me from the lust of wanting, grant me
This sadness always, continuance of this vision;
Stay with me, sorrow that is not sorrow but
The spring of all delight, of the troubled joy
Wherein I approach the consciousness of things
Yearning and aching always, and so become
Each day more closely bound to what you are.

Needham Cemetery

'A sightly place,' says Luke Orlando Ball
In *The History of Brome County*, 'sandy of soil,
Easy of access, level and well-drained.
You never saw the dead so well maintained.'
—Never, indeed: here corpses seldom spoil

Even in the wettest year—and this means much
To folk who raise their eyes to heaven but keep
Their feet upon the dear familiar ground
Which wears them out, as they go round and round
And to and fro: a kind of thinking sheep.

So slow to grasp, they like the second look,
So short of sight, they favour the long view;
And all that happens is that, right or wrong,
One comes too late, the other takes too long:
Time led them here, as it was bound to do....

As it was bound to do. And still the dead
Lecture their children on the way to live;
For the blood's didactic can perpetuate
Their useless virtues which are out of date,
Their antique vices which we half forgive.

Draw close, lean down, let the communal voice
Of a long-buried elder testify
Out of the soil he thought of first and last
(Bating his little leisure, which was passed
In waiting for his enemies to die):

Mind your own business. Owe no man a cent.
Keep out of trouble and away from war.
Don't trust a Frenchman. Be nobody's fool:
Nothing for nothing is the golden rule;
God lives in walls, the devil keeps the door.

'Look to the end. Pride goes before a fall.
The one mistake, remember, is to grow
Too big for your breeches: that's where Agag dulled
And how the tipsy Amalekites got fooled;
Jezebel flew high: she landed low.

'All flesh is grass: so keep the meadows up,
The hired man down, the women in their place;
Let your whole life turn with the turning year,
Obedient to the seasons. Have no fear
Lest hardness hood your eyes or twist your face,

'For sweet goes bad, but sour goes on forever ...
So look at your feet, your fields, the things you own,
And find God's meaning there: cows in the barn,
Crop in the mow and taxes paid. The farm,
The farm is the whole of life — what death alone

'Can take from you, giving himself instead
In whom its guardian and its genius move,
So interwoven is the daily round
— Dust in the air and silence underground —
That out of him you make your second love.'

Such counsels of perfection I have heard
In the autumn wind that sighs above these stones
Covered with angels, roses, pointing hands,
Witnessing what life gives and death demands
On a dry hillside full of farmers' bones.

The Cardinal's Dog

(Musée d'Autun)

The unknown Master of Moulins
Painted the Nativity: we see
The stable, the stupid ox and Mary,
Simpering Joseph on his knees
And the Cardinal Rolin on his knees too,
His red robe centred by a rat-faced dog.

They all look at each other: Joseph at Mary,
Mary (her face is blue) at the child,
The Cardinal looks, if anywhere, at the ox;
But the child looks at the little dog,
And the dog at nothing, simply being well-behaved:
He is the one who feels and knows....

Pensive little dog (you that I love
Being only flesh and blood) you see
The reason for all this, the dying need
Of the worshipful, the master: so
We are all one, have seen the birth of God

Either through eyes of friend or master,
In a book, a song, a landscape or a child,
For a breath of time are immortal, tuned
To the chord and certainties of animal hope.
And the picture *teaches* us—as Balzac would say—
To trust anything on earth more than man.

Thomas à Kempis

His unsubsistent mind, self-moving and
Subject to *rerum horror*, could observe
—Before its descent into the nightly grave—
Not that the cell expands, but the prisoner
Diminishes himself, not that he's brave,
But that, on earth, there's nothing left to fear.
Nobodaddy held him in his hand,

A fireless particle. I think we are
Coals ever cooling, blown at times by God;
And whether to strike or suffer for the good
Of all that breath has meant divides my hours,
And though to strike, to inch the door abroad,
Is all my vision allows (that—merciful powers!—
Confounds the firefly and the falling star),

The stroke or sufferance in the midnight is
An orchestral sigh. Always the cell is here,
Stronger than fire, than the release of fear,
Than any love that I can answer for....
But oh, green leaves and singing birds that see
The flaming sun, lie, lie of the open door,
The air of that bright heaven that is not his!

Utrillo's World

I

He sat above it, watching it recede,
A world of love resolved to empty spaces,
Streets without figures, figures without faces,
Desolate by choice and negative from need.
But the hoardings weep, the shutters burn and bleed;
Colours of crucifixion, dying graces,
Spatter and cling upon these sorrowful places.
—Where is the loved one? Where do the streets lead?

There is no loved one. Perfect fear
Has cast out love. And the streets go on forever
To blest annihilation, silently ascend
To their own assumption of bright points in air.
It is the world that counts, the endless fever,
And suffering that is its own and only end.

II

Anguished these sombre houses, still, resigned.
Suffering has found no better face than wood
For its own portrait, nor are tears so good
As the last reticence of being blind.
Grief without voice, mourning without mind,
I find your silence in this neighbourhood
Whose hideous buildings ransom with their blood
The shame and the self-loathing of mankind.

They are also masks that misery has put on
Over the faces and the festivals:
Madness and fear must have a place to hide,
And murder a secret room to call his own.
I know they are prisons also, these thin walls
Between us and what cowers and shakes inside.

Brummell at Calais

A foolish useless man who had done nothing
All his life long but keep himself clean,
Locked in the glittering armour of a pose
Made up of impudence, chastity and reserve —
How does his memory still survive his world?

The portraits show us only a tilted nose,
Lips full blown, a cravat and curly wig,
And a pair of posturing eyes,
Infinitely vulnerable, deeply innocent,
Their malice harmless as a child's:

And he has returned to childhood now, his stature
That of the Butterfly whose *Funeral*
He sang (his only song) for one of his
Dear duchesses, Frances or Georgiana,
In the intolerable metre of Tom Moore —

To a childhood of sweet biscuits and curaçao;
Hair-oil and tweezers make him forget his debts,
The angle of his hat remains the same,
His little boots pick their way over the cobblestones,
But where is he going as well as going mad?

Nowhere: his glory is already upon him,
The fading Regency man who will leave behind
More than the ankle-buttoning pantaloon!
For see, even now in the long implacable twilight,
The triumph of his veritable art,

An art of being, nothing but being, the grace
Of perfect self-assertion based on nothing,
As in our vanity's cause against the void
He strikes his elegant blow, the solemn report of those
Who have done nothing and will never die.

Fly in Autumn

Here he is, the loathsome one
Pushing from a crack in the window,
Fat with unseasonable seed, making his way
Towards the light of the dying year,

Washing his hands wearily, bemused
By the fictive summer of the house,
Driven from sleep by his god,
Feeling for his destiny.

Where are his parents, those spry lechers
Of a summer of roses and wine?
Papery corpses crumbling. Their bloated child
Stalks the failing sun.

Beelzebub, Prince of this World,
Is this not your servant in whom you were well pleased,
Now beloved of none, and sick?
Worthless one, Prince of this World …

Maggot, call on a greater god today:
Mercy, mercy, avert your lethal finger!
Let me *but live* to *suffer the frost,*
The slower death accessible to *all.*

A Point of Sky

Boredom, disaster and distress
Make the same furrows in the face,
The affections find a common line
Between mouth and eyebrow: the mirror
Has told you so. And today, in prison,
You are sad with the weight of a moment
Suddenly descended, simply to remember
What you were, reflect on what you are,
On time's reverses, and what brought you here
(Which is anywhere: this room and mountain, this rainy day)
To a kind of stopping-place, a centre
In the midst of a maze, and what makes you pause
And stare into the quiet rain
With all its millions of descending points,
Into all that fluency from this point of rest.
      So it happens, from time to time,
The suspended sentence falling on us like a fist,
The shape of blackness into which we are always moving:
Not the sudden, shattering terror
With something of the divine in it, which is
A certain contact and connection with God,
But the descent of the terrible clarity of tedium,
The vision of the true face of our condition,
The man in the mirror who is always there.

A house is falling
A dog is dying
A bird is singing
A woman is crying
A window is open
But air will not enter
There is no communion
Of settling and death
Of song and sorrow
Only the whirring
Of weights in a circle

A winking of lights
A passage of bodies
A cry in the darkness
As the world turns over

And you thought there would always be time,
Occasions to seize the occasion, combine the elements
Dazzle your own eyes with the work,
But there is no time;
In this hour the future has suddenly shrunken
Into the compass of the catoptric past,
Caught and pinned in a single glance
In this moment of inalterable vision,
Of sense and hearing sharpened to an agonized awareness
Of the tick of time when there is no time,
Of the pulse of life when life has been abolished.
You thought there would always be time
To arrange matters, to set the metals in order.
You thought there would always be life
And now there is only the flaming circle
Moving in aimless waves,
A disturbance of fire troubling the stillness.
Was there ever time? And the question raises
The question of a possible excuse
For what was left undone, the turning not taken,
The hardness not embraced, for the choice of a meadow
Drowsing in a white light of happiness,
A choice of the gate into that meadow and that light
Rather than the dark road ascending
Between the violet buildings, up and up
Towards an infinitesimal point of sky.
Who is to say there was never time nor occasion?
Only the demon who stands behind the shoulder,
The dark one, the unanswerable,
Who knows best, who is always right,
The master of salutary denials.

—No, there was never a choice
Of a turning towards the hard blue point of sky!
For even the future is only in the present,
Its hopes and terrors are here and now
And our pleasure and our death
Are consummated every day:
We are already happy
We are already dying
In the moment of speculation
Which holds the shape of the beauty and terror of the experience,
The haze and the storm,
In the moment which holds all our knowledge
As the poise and strain of pleasure is held in the beloved's mouth,
As her glance in the morning of meeting
Holds the whole history of our passion
Multiplying and making rich the events
That will never arrive.

In this moment
Of rest, this halting
Of hope and memory
Of all things falling
Away from the body,
Of a drift of silence
Upon all feeling,
With the rain falling
Between the spaces
Upon the vision
Of all things, halting
The mind's motion
Stopping the springs,
Think of the refuge,
The point of sky,

The certain castle,
The certain presence
Behind the appearance shaling, shaling
In pieces and powder.

Press with both hands the walls on either side
Bear up against the dark and descending vault
For the meadow has vanished and the point of sky also
Memory alone has built them into your mind
With their essence caught in the odour of clover
And in the sound of a clean blue wind blowing —
They are only the last of the inviolacies
You take with you into this little room
The prison and refuge of your life's remains.
Strive with both hands against the encroaching dark
Blow with your breath against the eructations
Deny, always deny that you are diminishing
Let your words burst like blisters in the face of the law
Asserting always it was not made for you.
Stop your ears against the beloved and sickly intimations
The slurred passage of slippered feet passing your door
Only to pass, never to pause
To pass on to a further door
Leading away to landings, stairs
And passages past other doors
Those tired restless feet never to halt
To be followed by no knocking
No visitation or communication
Only passing along and away —
Fight with both hands against the prison of God
And against the prison of time and eternal power
Let not your hands fail nor your desperation weaken
Against the warders who have shut the sky against you

That my regrets
May so shine before me
All the hours of my life
That I shall not sleep, and my eyes open
That I shall not die, and my heart beating
But shall remember always
The point of sky and the meadow
The thing foregone and the thing achieved
So that the beauty of both is united
In one clear flame of longing.

About John Glassco

John Glassco was born in Montreal on December 15, 1909. Two years after enrolling at McGill University, he abandoned his studies and, at seventeen, fled to Paris with his friend Graeme Taylor. The account of their adventures among the city's expat literary community appeared in *Memoirs of Montparnasse* (which, although written following his return to Canada in 1931, wasn't published until 1970).

In the late 1930s, Glassco and Taylor lived together in Quebec's Eastern Townships, settling first in the town of Knowlton and then, in the 1950s, in Foster. While trying to make headway on his prose and poetry, Glassco ran the rural mail route, founded the Foster Horse Show and eventually served as mayor of Foster. Taylor's death in 1957 spurred Glassco to return, with greater determination, to his writing. He grew close to the Montreal Group, a literary circle that included poets F.R. Scott and A.J.M. Smith. *The Deficit Made Flesh* (1958), his first book of poetry, was followed by *A Point of Sky* (1964) and *Selected Poems* (1971), which won the Governor General's Literary Award. *Montreal* (1973), a twenty-three-page poem, was his last volume of verse.

In 1963, he organized the Foster Poetry Conference, which remains one of the biggest gatherings of Quebec's English-language poets. Attendees included Irving Layton, Ralph Gustafson and Leonard Cohen. Originally intended as a bilingual celebration, Glassco's plans were scuttled after a series of bombings by Quebec separatists made inviting Francophone poets politically untenable. Inspired by Scott's efforts at translating French-Canadian poetry, Glassco devoted himself to translation, with his work collected in *The Journal of Saint-Denys Garneau* (1962), *Complete Poems of Saint-Denys Garneau* (1975) and the anthology *The Poetry of French Canada in Translation* (1970). Glassco's oeuvre also includes pseudonymous pornography. Some of the highlights of his self-described 'aphrodisiac works' were the sadomasochistic bestseller *The English Governess* (1960), published in Paris by the infamous Olympia Press, and *The Temple of Pederasty* (1970), which was banned.

Glassco died in Montreal in 1981, survived by his second wife, Marion McCormick. His ashes were thrown into a stream near his old home in Foster, Quebec.

Selected Bibliography

POETRY

The Deficit Made Flesh. (McClelland and Stewart, 1958).
A Point of Sky. (Oxford University Press, 1964).
Selected Poems. (Oxford University Press, 1971).
Squire Hardman. By George Colman. [pseud.] (Pastime Press, 1966).
Montreal. (DC Books, 1973).

PROSE

Under the Hill. By Aubrey Beardsley, completed by John Glassco. (Olympia Press, 1959).
The English Governess. By Miles Underwood [pseud.]. (Olympia Press, 1960).
English Poetry in Quebec. Proceedings of the Foster Poetry Conference 12–14, 1963. Edited by John Glassco. (McGill University Press, 1965).
Memoirs of Montparnasse. (Oxford University Press, 1970).
The Temple of Pederasty. Introduction by John Glassco. (Hanover House, 1970).
The Fatal Woman. Three tales by John Glassco. (House of Anansi, 1974).

TRANSLATION

The Journal of Saint-Denys Garneau. (McClelland and Stewart, 1962).
The Poetry of French Canada in Translation. Edited and Introduced by John Glassco. (Oxford University Press, 1970).
Complete Poems of Saint-Denys Garneau. (Oberon Press, 1975).
Lot's Wife. By Monique Bosco. (McClelland and Stewart, 1975).
Venus in Furs. Translated from the German by John Glassco. (Blackfish Press, 1977).
Creatures of the Chase. By Jean-Yves Soucy. (McClelland and Stewart, 1979).
Fear's Folly (Les demi-civilisées). By Jean-Charles Harvey. (Carleton University Press, 1982).